# All of Me

## arranged for harp by Sylvia Woods

### Words and Music by
### John Stephens and Toby Gad

# All of Me

Words and Music by John Stephens and Toby Gad
Harp Arrangement by Sylvia Woods

Moderately, with feeling

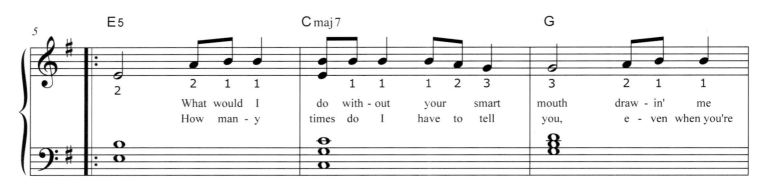

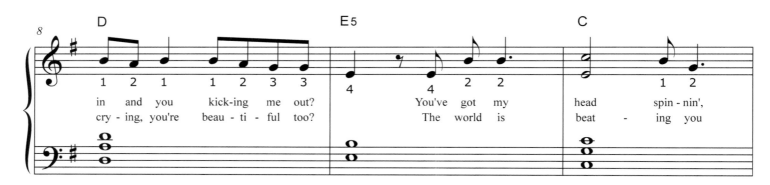

* may be played with right hand for page turn

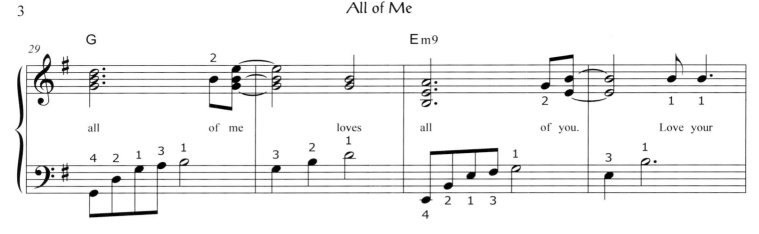

all of me loves all of you. Love your

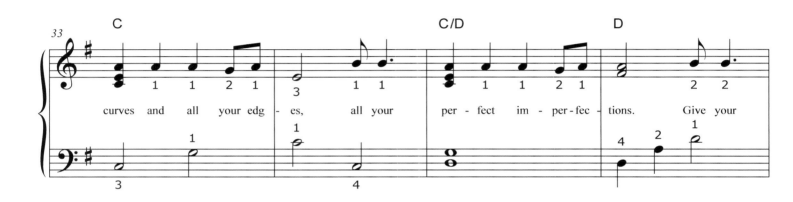

curves and all your edg - es, all your per - fect im - per - fec - tions. Give your

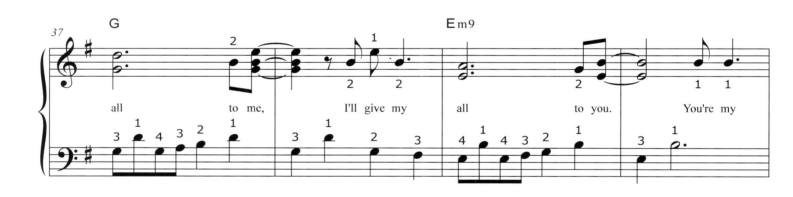

all to me, I'll give my all to you. You're my

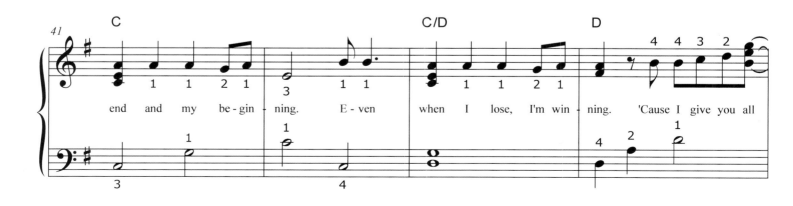

end and my be - gin - ning. E - ven when I lose, I'm win - ning. 'Cause I give you all

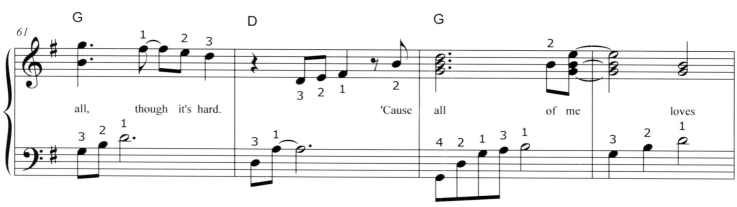

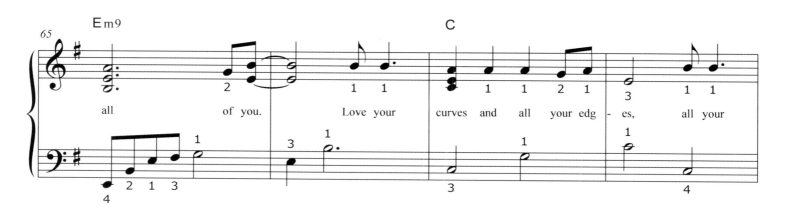

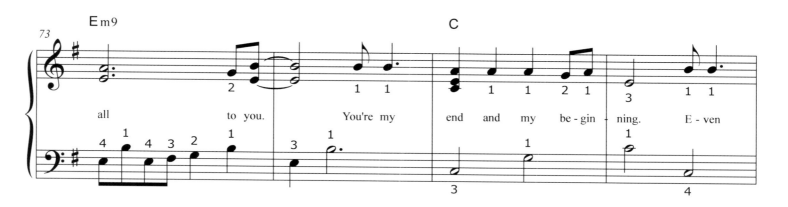

* If your harp doesn't have the high A string needed in measure 87, you may omit this note.

# All of Me

Grammy-winning R&B recording artist John Legend (John Roger Stephens) wrote this love ballad for his fiancée Chrissy Teigen. It was released in August 2013 as a single on his <u>Love in the Future</u> album. The couple married one month later. *All of Me* reached number one on the *Billboard Hot 100 Chart* in May, 2014.

---

# More Harp Arrangements of Pop Music by Sylvia Woods

Beauty and the Beast
Music from Disney-Pixar's <u>Brave</u>
Bring Him Home from <u>Les Misérables</u>
Castle on a Cloud from <u>Les Misérables</u>
A Charlie Brown Christmas
Dead Poets Society
John Denver Love Songs
76 Disney Songs
Fields of Gold
Fireflies
Music from Disney <u>Frozen</u>
Groovy Songs of the 60s
Four Holiday Favorites
House at Pooh Corner

Into the West from <u>The Lord of the Rings</u>
Lennon and McCartney
My Heart Will Go On from <u>Titanic</u>
Over the Rainbow from <u>The Wizard of Oz</u>
River Flows in You
22 Romantic Songs
Safe & Sound
Say Something
Stairway to Heaven
Music from Disney <u>Tangled</u>
A Thousand Years
Andrew Lloyd Webber Music
The Wizard of Oz
Theme from Disney-Pixar's <u>Up</u>

## Available from harp music retailers and www.harpcenter.com

**Sylvia Woods Harp Center**
P.O. Box 223434, Princeville, HI 96722 U.S.A.

U.S. $8.99

8 88680 02555 7

HL00131540

ISBN 978-0-936661-65-0

9 780936 661650

EXCLUSIVELY DISTRIBUTED BY

HAL•LEONARD
CORPORATION
7777 W. BLUEMOUND RD. P.O. BOX 13819
MILWAUKEE, WISCONSIN 53213

With many thanks to Paul Baker

© 2014 by Sylvia Woods
Published by Woods Music & Books
P.O. Box 223434, Princeville, HI 96722, U.S.A.
www.harpcenter.com